Resolve to Gain the Victory over Your Own Selves

A COMPILATION FROM THE BAHÁ'Í SACRED WRITINGS

TABLE OF CONTENTS

Introduction

The majority of the material presented in this compilation is comprised of passages from the Writings of Bahá'u'lláh, with one text from the Báb, some from 'Abdu'l-Bahá, one passage from a letter written on behalf of Shoghi Effendi, and one appendix from a letter written on behalf of the Universal House of Justice. It was compiled with an intentional sequence of correlated passages that would be conducive to spiritual growth, and not meant to be focused on elucidation of independent subjects.

For this reason, this material does not follow the ranking protocol that should be adopted when compiling Writings of the Faith. Indeed one will easily find passages that are not directly related to a theme under which they have been placed. In addition, of course, if one seeks to better understand a specific passage, it is advisable to refer back to the source from which the passage was extracted and study it in its broader context, using cross-references, and so forth.

'WORLDLINESS IN ITS ESSENCE'

Purge your hearts from love of the world, and your tongues from calumny, and your limbs from whatsoever may withhold you from drawing nigh unto God, the Mighty, the All-Praised. Say: By the world is meant that which turneth you aside from Him Who is the Dawning-Place of Revelation, and inclineth you unto that which is unprofitable unto you. Verily, the thing that deterreth you, in this day, from God is worldliness in its essence. Eschew it, and approach the Most Sublime Vision, this shining and resplendent Seat.

(Bahá'u'lláh, *Epistle to the Son of the Wolf,* p. 54)

Know ye that by "the world" is meant your unawareness of Him Who is your Maker, and your absorption in aught else but Him. The "life to come," on the other hand, signifieth the things that give you a safe approach to God, the All-Glorious, the Incomparable. Whatsoever deterreth you, in this Day, from loving God is nothing but the world. Flee it, that ye may be numbered with the blest. Should a man wish to adorn himself with the ornaments of the earth, to wear its apparels, or partake of the benefits it can bestow, no harm can befall him, if he alloweth nothing whatever to intervene between him and God, for God hath ordained every good thing, whether created in the heavens or in the earth, for such of His servants as truly believe in Him. Eat ye, O people, of the good things which God hath allowed you, and deprive not yourselves from His wondrous bounties. Render thanks and praise unto Him, and be of them that are truly thankful.

(Bahá'u'lláh, *Gleanings from the Writings of Bahá'u'lláh,* p. 275)

The Bird of the Realm of Utterance voiceth continually this call: "All things have I willed for thee, and thee, too, for thine own sake."

(Bahá'u'lláh, *Gleanings from the Writings of Bahá'u'lláh,* p. 259)

The world is continually proclaiming these words: Beware, I am evanescent, and so are all my outward appearances and colours. Take ye heed of the changes and chances contrived within me and be ye roused from your slumber. Nevertheless there is no discerning eye to see, nor is there a hearing ear to hearken.

(Bahá'u'lláh, *Tablets of Bahá'u'lláh*, p. 257 258)

By the righteousness of God! The world and its vanities, and its glory, and whatever delights it can offer, are all, in the sight of God, as worthless as, nay, even more contemptible than, dust and ashes. Would that the hearts of men could comprehend it! Cleanse yourselves thoroughly, O people of Bahá, from the defilement of the world, and of all that pertaineth unto it. God Himself beareth Me witness. The things of the earth ill beseem you. Cast them away unto such as may desire them, and fasten your eyes upon this most holy and effulgent Vision.

(Bahá'u'lláh, *Gleanings from the Writings of Bahá'u'lláh*, p. 304)

Know ye that the world and its vanities and its embellishments shall pass away. Nothing will endure except God's Kingdom which pertaineth to none but Him, the Sovereign Lord of all, the Help in Peril, the All-Glorious, the Almighty. The days of your life shall roll away, and all the things with which ye are occupied and of which ye boast yourselves shall perish, and ye shall, most certainly, be summoned by a company of His angels to appear at the spot where the limbs of the entire creation shall be made to tremble, and the flesh of every oppressor to creep. Ye shall be asked of the things your hands have wrought in this, your vain life, and shall be repaid for your doings. This is the day that shall inevitably come upon you, the hour that none can put back. To this the Tongue of Him that speaketh the truth and is the Knower of all things hath testified.

(Bahá'u'lláh, *Gleanings from the Writings of Bahá'u'lláh*, p. 123)

O ye loved ones of God! Know ye that the world is even as a mirage rising over the sands, that the thirsty mistaketh for water. The wine of this world is but a vapour in the desert, its pity and compassion but toil and trouble, the repose it proffereth only weariness and sorrow. Abandon it to those who belong to it, and turn your faces unto the Kingdom of your Lord the All-Merciful, that His grace and bounty may cast their dawning splendours over you, and a heavenly table may be sent down for you, and your Lord may bless you, and shower His riches upon you to gladden your bosoms and fill your hearts with bliss, to attract your minds, and cleanse your souls, and console your eyes.

('Abdu'l-Bahá, *Selections from the Writings of 'Abdu'l-Bahá*, p. 186)

O YE THAT PRIDE YOURSELVES ON MORTAL RICHES! Know ye in truth that wealth is a mighty barrier between the seeker and his desire, the lover and his beloved. The rich, but for a few, shall in no wise attain the court of His presence nor enter the city of content and resignation. Well is it then with him, who, being rich, is not hindered by his riches from the eternal kingdom, nor deprived by them of imperishable dominion. By the Most Great Name! The splendor of such a wealthy man shall illuminate the dwellers of heaven even as the sun enlightens the people of the earth!

(Bahá'u'lláh, *The Hidden Words*, Persian #53)

Wealth is praiseworthy in the highest degree, if it is acquired by an individual's own efforts and the grace of God, in commerce, agriculture, art and industry, and if it be expended for philanthropic purposes. Above all, if a judicious and resourceful individual should initiate measures which would universally enrich the masses of the people, there could be no undertaking greater than this, and it would rank in the sight of God as the supreme achievement, for such a benefactor would supply the needs and insure the comfort and well-being of a great multitude. Wealth is most commendable, provided the entire population is wealthy. If, however, a few have inordinate riches while the rest are impoverished, and no fruit or benefit accrues from that wealth, then it is only a liability to its possessor. If, on the other hand, it is expended for the promotion of knowledge, the founding of elementary and other schools, the encouragement of art and industry, the training of orphans and the poor -- in brief, if it is dedicated to the welfare of society -- its possessor will stand out before God and man as the most excellent of all who live on earth and will be accounted as one of the people of paradise.

('Abdu'l-Bahá, *The Secret of Divine Civilization*, p. 24-5)

O SON OF BEING! Busy not thyself with this world, for with fire We test the gold, and with gold We test Our servants.

(Bahá'u'lláh, *The Hidden Words*, Arabic #55)

We see you rejoicing in that which ye have amassed for others and shutting out yourselves from the worlds which naught except My guarded Tablet can reckon. The treasures ye have laid up have drawn you far away from your ultimate objective. This ill beseemeth you, could ye but understand it. Wash your hearts from all earthly defilements, and hasten to enter the Kingdom of your Lord, the Creator of earth and heaven, Who caused the world to tremble and all its peoples to wail, except them that have renounced all things and clung to that which the Hidden Tablet hath ordained.

(Bahá'u'lláh, *Gleanings from the Writings of Bahá'u'lláh*, p. 210)

Exultest thou over the treasures thou dost possess, knowing they shall perish? Rejoicest thou in that thou rulest a span of earth, when the whole world, in the estimation of the people of Bahá, is worth as much as the black in the eye of a dead ant? Abandon it unto such as have set their affections upon it, and turn thou unto Him Who is the Desire of the world. Whither are gone the proud and their palaces? Gaze thou into their tombs, that thou mayest profit by this example, inasmuch as We made it a lesson unto every beholder. Were the breezes of Revelation to seize thee, thou wouldst flee the world, and turn unto the Kingdom, and wouldst expend all thou possessest, that thou mayest draw nigh unto this sublime Vision.

(Bahá'u'lláh, *The Summons of the Lord of Hosts*, p. 81)

O YE THAT ARE LYING AS DEAD ON THE COUCH OF HEEDLESSNESS! Ages have passed and your precious lives are well-nigh ended, yet not a single breath of purity hath reached Our court of holiness from you. Though immersed in the ocean of misbelief, yet with your lips ye profess the one true faith of God. Him whom I abhor ye have loved, and of My foe ye have made a friend. Notwithstanding, ye walk on My earth complacent and self-satisfied, heedless that My earth is weary of you and everything within it shunneth you. Were ye but to open your eyes, ye would, in truth, prefer a myriad griefs unto this joy, and would count death itself better than this life.

(Bahá'u'lláh, *The Hidden Words*, Persian #20)

If true glory were to consist in the possession of such perishable things, then the earth on which ye walk must needs vaunt itself over you, because it supplieth you, and bestoweth upon you, these very things, by the decree of the Almighty. In its bowels are contained, according to what God hath ordained, all that ye possess. From it, as a sign of His mercy, ye derive your riches. Behold then your state, the thing in which ye glory! Would that ye could perceive it!

(Bahá'u'lláh, *The Summons of the Lord of Hosts*, p. 190)

Every man of discernment, while walking upon the earth, feeleth indeed abashed, inasmuch as he is fully aware that the thing which is the source of his prosperity, his wealth, his might, his exaltation, his advancement and power is, as ordained by God, the very earth which is trodden beneath the feet of all men. There can be no doubt that whoever is cognizant of this truth, is cleansed and sanctified from all pride, arrogance, and vainglory. Whatever hath been said hath come from God. Unto this, He, verily, hath borne, and beareth now, witness, and He, in truth, is the All-Knowing, the All-Informed.

(Bahá'u'lláh, *Epistle to the Son of the Wolf*, p. 44)

By God! In earthly riches fear is hidden and peril is concealed. Consider ye and call to mind that which the All-Merciful hath revealed in the Qur'án: 'Woe betide every slanderer and defamer, him that layeth up riches and counteth them.'[1] Fleeting are the riches of the world; all that perisheth and changeth is not, and hath never been, worthy of attention, except to a recognized measure.

[1 *Qur'án* 104:1-2.]
(Bahá'u'lláh, *Tablets of Bahá'u'lláh*, p. 217 219)

How great the multitude of the poor who have quaffed the choice wine of divine revelation and how many the rich who have turned away, repudiated the truth and voiced their disbelief in God, the Lord of this blessed and wondrous Day!

(Bahá'u'lláh, *Tablets of Bahá'u'lláh*, p. 248)

Say: O people! Let not this life and its deceits deceive you, for the world and all that is therein is held firmly in the grasp of His Will. He bestoweth His favor on whom He willeth, and from whom He willeth He taketh it away. He doth whatsoever He chooseth. Had the world been of any worth in His sight, He surely would never have allowed His enemies to possess it, even to the extent of a grain of mustard seed. He hath, however, caused you to be entangled with its affairs, in return for what your hands have wrought in His Cause. This, indeed, is a chastisement which ye, of your own will, have inflicted upon yourselves, could ye but perceive it. Are ye rejoicing in the things which, according to the estimate of God, are contemptible and worthless, things wherewith He proveth the hearts of the doubtful?

(Bahá'u'lláh, *Gleanings from the Writings of Bahá'u'lláh*, p. 207)

For after all, the earth is but the everlasting graveyard, the vast, universal cemetery of all mankind. Yet men fight to possess this graveyard, waging war and battle, killing each other. What ignorance! How spacious the earth is with room in plenty for all! How thoughtful the providence which has so allotted that every man may derive his sustenance from it! The Lord, our Creator, does not ordain that anyone should starve or live in want. All are intended to participate in the blessed and abundant bestowals of our God. Fundamentally, all warfare and bloodshed in the human world are due to the lack of unity between the religions, which through superstitions and

adherence to theological dogmas have obscured the one reality
which is the source and basis of them all.

('Abdu'l-Bahá, *The Promulgation of Universal Peace*, p. 395)

Say: O people! Withhold not from yourselves the grace of
God and His mercy. Whoso withholdeth himself therefrom is
indeed in grievous loss. What, O people! Do ye worship the
dust, and turn away from your Lord, the Gracious, the All-
Bountiful? Fear ye God, and be not of those who perish.

(Bahá'u'lláh, *Gleanings from the Writings of Bahá'u'lláh*, p. 104)

Where is he to be found who, through the power of My
name that transcendeth all created things, will cast away the
things that men possess, and cling, with all his might, to the
things which God, the Knower of the unseen and of the seen,
hath bidden him observe? Thus hath His bounty been sent
down unto men, His testimony fulfilled, and His proof shone
forth above the Horizon of mercy. Rich is the prize that shall
be won by him who hath believed and exclaimed: "Lauded
art Thou, O Beloved of all worlds! Magnified be Thy name, O
Thou the Desire of every understanding heart!

(Bahá'u'lláh, *Gleanings from the Writings of Bahá'u'lláh*, p. 34)

O SON OF THE SUPREME! To the eternal I call thee,
yet thou dost seek that which perisheth. What hath made thee
turn away from Our desire and seek thine own?

(Bahá'u'lláh, *The Hidden Words*, Arabic #23)

O SON OF MAN! Thou dost wish for gold and I desire
thy freedom from it. Thou thinkest thyself rich in its possession, and I recognize thy wealth in thy sanctity therefrom. By
My life! This is My knowledge, and that is thy fancy; how can
My way accord with thine?

(Bahá'u'lláh, *The Hidden Words*, Arabic #56)

The days of your life are far spent, O people, and your end is fast approaching. Put away, therefore, the things ye have devised and to which ye cleave, and take firm hold on the precepts of God, that haply ye may attain that which He hath purposed for you, and be of them that pursue a right course. Delight not yourselves in the things of the world and its vain ornaments, neither set your hopes on them. Let your reliance be on the remembrance of God, the Most Exalted, the Most Great. He will, erelong, bring to naught all the things ye possess. Let Him be your fear, and forget not His covenant with you, and be not of them that are shut out as by a veil from Him.

(Bahá'u'lláh, *Gleanings from the Writings of Bahá'u'lláh*, p. 127)

Walk not in the paths of the Evil One. Walk ye, during the few remaining days of your life, in the ways of the one true God. Your days shall pass away as have the days of them who were before you. To dust shall ye return, even as your fathers of old did return.

(Bahá'u'lláh, *Gleanings from the Writings of Bahá'u'lláh*, p. 125)

Take heed lest pride deter you from recognizing the Source of Revelation, lest the things of this world shut you out as by a veil from Him Who is the Creator of heaven.

(Bahá'u'lláh, *Gleanings from the Writings of Bahá'u'lláh*, p. 211)

O SON OF SPIRIT! The bird seeketh its nest; the nightingale the charm of the rose; whilst those birds, the hearts of men, content with transient dust, have strayed far from their eternal nest, and with eyes turned towards the slough of heedlessness are bereft of the glory of the divine presence. Alas! How strange and pitiful; for a mere cupful, they have turned away from the billowing seas of the Most High, and remained far from the most effulgent horizon.

(Bahá'u'lláh, *The Hidden Words*, Persian #2)

O FRIENDS! Abandon not the everlasting beauty for a beauty that must die, and set not your affections on this mortal world of dust.

(Bahá'u'lláh, *The Hidden Words*, Persian #14)

O MY SERVANT! Abandon not for that which perisheth an everlasting dominion, and cast not away celestial sovereignty for a worldly desire. This is the river of everlasting life that hath flowed from the well-spring of the pen of the merciful; well is it with them that drink!

(Bahá'u'lláh, *The Hidden Words*, Persian #37)

O OFFSPRING OF DUST! Be not content with the ease of a passing day, and deprive not thyself of everlasting rest. Barter not the garden of eternal delight for the dust-heap of a mortal world. Up from thy prison ascend unto the glorious meads above, and from thy mortal cage wing thy flight unto the paradise of the Placeless.

(Bahá'u'lláh, *The Hidden Words*, Persian #39)

O CHILDREN OF VAINGLORY! For a fleeting sovereignty ye have abandoned My imperishable dominion, and have adorned yourselves with the gay livery of the world and made of it your boast. By My beauty! All will I gather beneath the one-colored covering of the dust and efface all these diverse colors save them that choose My own, and that is purging from every color.

(Bahá'u'lláh, *The Hidden Words*, Persian #74)

The peoples of the world are fast asleep. Were they to wake from their slumber, they would hasten with eagerness unto God, the All-Knowing, the All-Wise. They would cast away everything they possess, be it all the treasures of the earth, that their Lord may remember them to the extent of addressing to them but one word.

(Bahá'u'lláh, *The Kitáb-i-Aqdas,* p. 33)

Yet it behoveth the people of truth that the signs of humility should shine upon their faces, that the light of sanctity should radiate from their countenances, that they should walk upon the earth as though they were in the presence of God and distinguish themselves in their deeds from all the dwellers of the earth. Such must be their state that their eyes should behold the evidences of His might, their tongues and hearts make mention of His name, their feet be set towards the lands of His nearness, and their hands take fast hold upon His precepts. And were they to pass through a valley of pure gold and mines of precious silver, they should regard them as wholly unworthy of their attention.

(Bahá'u'lláh, *Gems of Divine Mysteries,* p. 59)

Man's merit lieth in service and virtue and not in the pageantry of wealth and riches. Take heed that your words be purged from idle fancies and worldly desires and your deeds be cleansed from craftiness and suspicion. Dissipate not the wealth of your precious lives in the pursuit of evil and corrupt affection, nor let your endeavours be spent in promoting your personal interest. Be generous in your days of plenty, and be patient in the hour of loss. Adversity is followed by success and rejoicings follow woe. Guard against idleness and sloth, and cling unto that which profiteth mankind, whether young or old, whether high or low. Beware lest ye sow tares of dissension among men or plant thorns of doubt in pure and radiant hearts.

(Bahá'u'lláh, Tablets of Bahá'u'lláh, p. 138)

'Self and Passion'

Thou hast asked Me concerning the nature of the soul. Know, verily, that the soul is a sign of God, a heavenly gem whose reality the most learned of men hath failed to grasp, and whose mystery no mind, however acute, can ever hope to unravel. It is the first among all created things to declare the excellence of its Creator, the first to recognize His glory, to cleave to His truth, and to bow down in adoration before Him. If it be faithful to God, it will reflect His light, and will, eventually, return unto Him. If it fails, however, in its allegiance to its Creator, it will become a victim to self and passion, and will, in the end, sink in their depths.

(Bahá'u'lláh, *Gleanings from the Writings of Bahá'u'lláh*, p. 158)

Know also that the soul is endowed with two wings: should it soar in the atmosphere of love and contentment, then it will be related to the All-Merciful. And should it fly in the atmosphere of self and desire, then it will pertain to the Evil One; may God shield and protect us and protect you therefrom, O ye who perceive! Should the soul become ignited with the fire of the love of God, it is called benevolent and pleasing unto God, but should it be consumed with the fire of passion, it is known as the concupiscent soul. Thus have We expounded this subject for thee that thou mayest obtain a clear understanding.

(Bahá'u'lláh, *The Summons of the Lord of Hosts*, p. 154)

The reality underlying this question is that the evil spirit, Satan or whatever is interpreted as evil, refers to the lower nature in man. This baser nature is symbolized in various ways. In man there are two expressions, one is the expression of nature, the other the expression of the spiritual realm. The world of nature is defective. Look at it clearly, casting aside all superstition and imagination. If you should leave a man uneducated and barbarous in the wilds of Africa, would there be any doubt about his remaining ignorant? God has never created an evil spirit; all such ideas and nomenclature are symbols expressing the mere human or earthly nature of man. It is an essential condition of the soil of earth that thorns, weeds and fruitless trees may grow from it. Relatively speaking, this is evil; it is simply the lower state and baser product of nature.

('Abdu'l-Bahá, *Foundations of World Unity*, p. 77)

Regarding the questions you asked: Self has really two meanings, or is used in two senses, in the Bahá'í writings; one is self, the identity of the individual created by God. This is the self mentioned in such passages as 'he hath known God who hath known himself etc.'. The other self is the ego, the dark, animalistic heritage each one of us has, the lower nature that can develop into a monster of selfishness, brutality, lust and so on. It is this self we must struggle against, or this side of our natures, in order to strengthen and free the spirit within us and help it to attain perfection.

Self-sacrifice means to subordinate this lower nature and its desires to the more godly and noble side of ourselves. Ultimately, in its highest sense, self-sacrifice means to give our will and our all to God to do with as He pleases. Then He purifies and glorifies our true self until it becomes a shining and wonderful reality.

(Compilations, *Lights of Guidance*, p. 113
From a letter written on behalf of Shoghi Effendi
to an individual believer, December 10, 1947)

This lower nature in man is symbolized as Satan -- the evil ego within us, not an evil personality outside.

('Abdu'l-Bahá, *The Promulgation of Universal Peace*, p. 286)

A man should pause and reflect and be just: his Lord, out of measureless grace, has made him a human being and honored him with the words: "Verily, We created man in the goodliest of forms"[1] -- and caused His mercy which rises out of the dawn of oneness to shine down upon him, until he became the wellspring of the words of God and the place where the mysteries of heaven alighted, and on the morning of creation he was covered with the rays of the qualities of perfection and the graces of holiness. How can he stain this immaculate garment with the filth of selfish desires, or exchange this everlasting honor for infamy? "Dost thou think thyself only a puny form, when the universe is folded up within thee?"[2]

[1 Qur'án 95:4.] [2 The Imam Ali.]
('Abdu'l-Bahá, *The Secret of Divine Civilization*, p. 19.)

The winds of self and passion move them as they will, and We found them all bereft of constancy.

(Bahá'u'lláh, *The Summons of the Lord of Hosts*, p. 94)

How very strange the imaginings of those who speak as prompted by their own caprices, and who wander distractedly in the wilderness of self and passion!

(Bahá'u'lláh, *The Summons of the Lord of Hosts*, p. 100)

The lowliest and most abject of all things holdeth sway over thee, and that is none other than self and passion, which have ever been reprehensible.

(Bahá'u'lláh, *The Summons of the Lord of Hosts*, p. 170)

Thus it is that certain invalid souls have confined the lands of knowledge within the wall of self and passion, and clouded them with ignorance and blindness, and have been veiled from the light of the mystic sun and the mysteries of the Eternal Beloved; they have strayed afar from the jewelled wisdom of

the lucid Faith of the Lord of Messengers, have been shut out
of the sanctuary of the All-Beauteous One, and banished from
the Ka'bih of splendor.

(Bahá'u'lláh, *The Seven Valleys*, p. 19)

Indeed the face of the sun of justice and fairness is hidden
behind the clouds of idle fancy which the foolish ones have
conceived.

(Bahá'u'lláh, *Tablets of Bahá'u'lláh*, p. 236)

Behold how the sun shines upon all creation, but only
surfaces that are pure and polished can reflect its glory and
light. The darkened soul has no portion of the revelation of the
glorious effulgence of reality; and the soil of self, unable to take
advantage of that light, does not produce growth.

('Abdu'l-Bahá, *The Promulgation of Universal Peace*, p. 148)

We have forbidden men to walk after the imaginations of
their hearts, that they may be enabled to recognize Him Who
is the sovereign Source and Object of all knowledge, and may
acknowledge whatsoever He may be pleased to reveal. Witness
how they have entangled themselves with their idle fancies and
vain imaginations. By My life! They are themselves the victims
of what their own hearts have devised, and yet they perceive
it not. Vain and profitless is the talk of their lips, and yet they
understand not.

(Bahá'u'lláh, *Gleanings from the Writings of Bahá'u'lláh*, p. 204)

Cast upon them, O My God, the glances of the eye of Thy
favour and bounty, and deliver them from self and passion,
that they may draw nigh unto Thy most exalted Horizon, taste
the sweetness of Thy remembrance, and delight in that bread

which Thou hast sent down from the heaven of Thy Will and
the firmament of Thy grace.

(Bahá'u'lláh, *The Summons of the Lord of Hosts*, p. 103)

They whom God hath endued with insight will readily recognize that the precepts laid down by God constitute the highest
means for the maintenance of order in the world and the securi-
ty of its peoples. He that turneth away from them, is accounted
among the abject and foolish. We, verily, have commanded you
to refuse the dictates of your evil passions and corrupt desires,
and not to transgress the bounds which the Pen of the Most
High hath fixed, for these are the breath of life unto all created
things. The seas of Divine wisdom and divine utterance have
risen under the breath of the breeze of the All-Merciful. Hasten to drink your fill, O men of understanding! They that have
violated the Covenant of God by breaking His commandments,
and have turned back on their heels, these have erred grievously
in the sight of God, the All-Possessing, the Most High.

(Bahá'u'lláh, *Gleanings from the Writings of Bahá'u'lláh*, p. 329)

Beware lest the desires of the flesh and of a corrupt inclina-
tion provoke divisions among you. Be ye as the fingers of one
hand, the members of one body. Thus counselleth you the Pen
of Revelation, if ye be of them that believe.

(Bahá'u'lláh, *The Kitáb-i-Aqdas*, p. 40)

It followeth, therefore, that rendering assistance unto God,
in this day, doth not and shall never consist in contending or
disputing with any soul; nay rather, what is preferable in the
sight of God is that the cities of men's hearts, which are ruled
by the hosts of self and passion, should be subdued by the
sword of utterance, of wisdom and of understanding.

(Bahá'u'lláh, *The Summons of the Lord of Hosts*, p. 109)

Every good thing is of God, and every evil thing is from yourselves. Will ye not comprehend?

(Bahá'u'lláh, *Gleanings from the Writings of Bahá'u'lláh,* p. 149)

Erelong the world and all that thou possessest will perish, and the kingdom will remain unto God, thy Lord and the Lord of thy fathers of old. It behooveth thee not to conduct thine affairs according to the dictates of thy desires.

(Bahá'u'lláh, *Epistle to the Son of the Wolf,* p. 50)

Obstruct not the luminous spring of thy soul with the thorns and brambles of vain and inordinate affections, and impede not the flow of the living waters that stream from the fountain of thine heart.

(Bahá'u'lláh, *Gleanings from the Writings of Bahá'u'lláh,* p. 323)

O SON OF BOUNTY! Out of the wastes of nothingness, with the clay of My command I made thee to appear, and have ordained for thy training every atom in existence and the essence of all created things. Thus, ere thou didst issue from thy mother's womb, I destined for thee two founts of gleaming milk, eyes to watch over thee, and hearts to love thee. Out of My loving-kindness, 'neath the shade of My mercy I nurtured thee, and guarded thee by the essence of My grace and favor. And My purpose in all this was that thou mightest attain My everlasting dominion and become worthy of My invisible bestowals. And yet heedless thou didst remain, and when fully grown, thou didst neglect all My bounties and occupied thyself with thine idle imaginings, in such wise that thou didst become wholly forgetful, and, turning away from the portals of the Friend didst abide within the courts of My enemy.

(Bahá'u'lláh, *The Hidden Words,* Persian #29)

O DWELLERS OF MY PARADISE! With the hands of loving-kindness I have planted in the holy garden of paradise the young tree of your love and friendship, and have watered it with the goodly showers of My tender grace; now that the hour of its fruiting is come, strive that it may be protected, and be not consumed with the flame of desire and passion.

(Bahá'u'lláh, *The Hidden Words*, Persian #34)

ALAS! ALAS! O LOVERS OF WORLDLY DESIRE! Even as the swiftness of lightning ye have passed by the Beloved One, and have set your hearts on satanic fancies. Ye bow the knee before your vain imagining, and call it truth. Ye turn your eyes towards the thorn, and name it a flower. Not a pure breath have ye breathed, nor hath the breeze of detachment been wafted from the meadows of your hearts. Ye have cast to the winds the loving counsels of the Beloved and have effaced them utterly from the tablet of your hearts, and even as the beasts of the field, ye move and have your being within the pastures of desire and passion.

(Bahá'u'lláh, *The Hidden Words*, Persian #45)

O WEED THAT SPRINGETH OUT OF DUST! Wherefore have not these soiled hands of thine touched first thine own garment, and why with thine heart defiled with desire and passion dost thou seek to commune with Me and to enter My sacred realm? Far, far are ye from that which ye desire.

(Bahá'u'lláh, *The Hidden Words*, Persian #68)

O CHILDREN OF NEGLIGENCE! Set not your affections on mortal sovereignty and rejoice not therein. Ye are even as the unwary bird that with full confidence warbleth upon the bough; till of a sudden the fowler Death throws it upon the dust, and the melody, the form and the color are gone, leaving not a trace. Wherefore take heed, O bondslaves of desire!

(Bahá'u'lláh, *The Hidden Words*, Persian #75)

O SON OF DESIRE! How long wilt thou soar in the realms of desire? Wings have I bestowed upon thee, that thou mayest fly to the realms of mystic holiness and not the regions of satanic fancy. The comb, too, have I given thee that thou mayest dress My raven locks, and not lacerate My throat.

(Bahá'u'lláh, *The Hidden Words*, Persian #79)

O SON OF MAN! Many a day hath passed over thee whilst thou hast busied thyself with thy fancies and idle imaginings. How long art thou to slumber on thy bed? Lift up thy head from slumber, for the Sun hath risen to the zenith, haply it may shine upon thee with the light of beauty.

(Bahá'u'lláh, *The Hidden Words*, Arabic #62)

'By the Power of God's Might, Resolve to Gain the Victory Over Your Own Selves'

Arise, O people, and, by the power of God's might, resolve
to gain the victory over your own selves, that haply the whole
earth may be freed and sanctified from its servitude to the gods
of its idle fancies -- gods that have inflicted such loss upon, and
are responsible for the misery of, their wretched worshipers.
These idols form the obstacle that impedeth man in his efforts
to advance in the path of perfection. We cherish the hope that
the Hand of Divine power may lend its assistance to mankind,
and deliver it from its state of grievous abasement.

In one of the Tablets these words have been revealed: O
people of God! Do not busy yourselves in your own concerns;
let your thoughts be fixed upon that which will rehabilitate
the fortunes of mankind and sanctify the hearts and souls of
men. This can best be achieved through pure and holy deeds,
through a virtuous life and a goodly behavior.

(Bahá'u'lláh, *Gleanings from the Writings of Bahá'u'lláh*, p. 93)

All that which ye potentially possess can, however, be
manifested only as a result of your own volition. Your own acts
testify to this truth.

(Bahá'u'lláh, *Gleanings from the Writings of Bahá'u'lláh*, p. 149)

There can be no doubt whatever that, in consequence of
the efforts which every man may consciously exert and as a
result of the exertion of his own spiritual faculties, this mirror
can be so cleansed from the dross of earthly defilements and
purged from satanic fancies as to be able to draw nigh unto the
meads of eternal holiness and attain the courts of everlasting
fellowship.

(Bahá'u'lláh, *Gleanings from the Writings of Bahá'u'lláh*, p. 262)

Success or failure, gain or loss, must, therefore, depend upon man's own exertions. The more he striveth, the greater will be his progress. We fain would hope that the vernal showers of the bounty of God may cause the flowers of true understanding to spring from the soil of men's hearts, and may wash them from all earthly defilements.

(Bahá'u'lláh, *Gleanings from the Writings of Bahá'u'lláh*, p. 81)

...man should know his own self and recognize that which leadeth unto loftiness or lowliness, glory or abasement, wealth or poverty.

(Bahá'u'lláh, *Tablets of Bahá'u'lláh*, p. 34 35)

The differences among mankind are of two sorts: one is a difference of station, and this difference is not blameworthy. The other is a difference of faith and assurance; the loss of these is blameworthy, for then the soul is overwhelmed by his desires and passions, which deprive him of these blessings and prevent him from feeling the power of attraction of the love of God. Though that man is praiseworthy and acceptable in his station, yet as he is deprived of the perfections of that degree, he will become a source of imperfections, for which he is held responsible. [1]

[1 Cf. "The Causes of Differences in the Characters of Men," p. 212.]

('Abdu'l-Bahá, *Some Answered Questions*, p. 129-130)

Arise and, armed with the power of faith, shatter to pieces the gods of your vain imaginings, the sowers of dissension amongst you.

(Bahá'u'lláh, *The Proclamation of Bahá'u'lláh*, p. 114)

We, verily, have commanded you to refuse the dictates of
your evil passions and corrupt desires, and not to transgress the
bounds which the Pen of the Most High hath fixed, for these
are the breath of life unto all created things.

(Bahá'u'lláh, *The Kitáb-i-Aqdas*, p. 19)

Then we must labor to destroy the animal condition, till
the meaning of humanity shall come to light.

(Bahá'u'lláh, *The Seven Valleys*, p. 34)

O Friends of the Pure and Omnipotent God! To be pure
and holy in all things is an attribute of the consecrated soul
and a necessary characteristic of the unenslaved mind. The best
of perfections is immaculacy and the freeing of oneself from
every defect. Once the individual is, in every respect, cleansed
and purified, then will he become a focal centre reflecting the
Manifest Light.

('Abdu'l-Bahá, *Selections from the Writings of 'Abdu'l-Bahá*, p. 146)

...rest ye not, seek ye no composure, attach not yourselves
to the luxuries of this ephemeral world, free yourselves from every attachment, and strive with heart and soul to become fully
established in the Kingdom of God.

('Abdu'l-Bahá, *Tablets of the Divine Plan*, p. 95 87)

We fain would hope that through thine exertions the wings
of men may be sanctified from the mire of self and desire,
and be made worthy to soar in the atmosphere of God's love.
Wings that are besmirched with mire can never soar. Unto this
testify they who are the exponents of justice and equity, and yet
the people are in evident doubt.

(Bahá'u'lláh, *Epistle to the Son of the Wolf*, p. 130)

He Who is the Day Spring of Truth is, no doubt, fully capable of rescuing from such remoteness wayward souls and of causing them to draw nigh unto His court and attain His Presence. "If God had pleased He had surely made all men one people." His purpose, however, is to enable the pure in spirit and the detached in heart to ascend, by virtue of their own innate powers, unto the shores of the Most Great Ocean, that thereby they who seek the Beauty of the All-Glorious may be distinguished and separated from the wayward and perverse. Thus hath it been ordained by the all-glorious and resplendent Pen....

(Bahá'u'lláh, *Gleanings from the Writings of Bahá'u'lláh*, p. 71)

Unto their sincerity hath borne witness what the All-Merciful hath sent down in the Qur'án. He saith: "Wish ye, then, for death, if ye are sincere." [1]

[1 Qur'án 2:88.]
(Bahá'u'lláh, *Tablets of Bahá'u'lláh*, p. 209)

O SON OF LOVE! Thou art but one step away from the glorious heights above and from the celestial tree of love. Take thou one pace and with the next advance into the immortal realm and enter the pavilion of eternity. Give ear then to that which hath been revealed by the pen of glory.

(Bahá'u'lláh, *The Hidden Words*, Persian #7)

'Cleanse from Your Hearts the Love of Worldly Things'

Cleanse from your hearts the love of worldly things, from your tongues every remembrance except His remembrance, from your entire being whatsoever may deter you from beholding His face, or may tempt you to follow the promptings of your evil and corrupt inclinations. Let God be your fear, O people, and be ye of them that tread the path of righteousness.

(Bahá'u'lláh, *Gleanings from the Writings of Bahá'u'lláh*, p. 274)

Say: Deliver your souls, O people, from the bondage of self, and purify them from all attachment to anything besides Me. Remembrance of Me cleanseth all things from defilement, could ye but perceive it. Say: Were all created things to be entirely divested of the veil of worldly vanity and desire, the Hand of God would in this Day clothe them, one and all, with the robe "He doeth whatsoever He willeth in the kingdom of creation," that thereby the sign of His sovereignty might be manifested in all things. Exalted then be He, the Sovereign Lord of all, the Almighty, the Supreme Protector, the All-Glorious, the Most Powerful.

(Bahá'u'lláh, *Gleanings from the Writings of Bahá'u'lláh*, p. 294)

...cleanse thine heart from the world and all its vanities, and suffer not the love of any stranger to enter and dwell therein. Not until thou dost purify thine heart from every trace of such love can the brightness of the light of God shed its radiance upon it, for to none hath God given more than one heart. This, verily, hath been decreed and written down in His ancient Book. And as the human heart, as fashioned by God, is one and undivided, it behoveth thee to take heed that its affections be, also, one and undivided. Cleave thou, therefore, with the whole affection of thine heart, unto His love, and withdraw it from the love of any one besides Him, that He may aid thee to immerse thyself in the ocean of His unity, and enable thee to become a true upholder of His oneness.

(Bahá'u'lláh, *Gleanings from the Writings of Bahá'u'lláh*, p. 237)

Would that the hearts of men could be cleansed from these man-made limitations and obscure thoughts imposed upon them! haply they may be illumined by the light of the Sun of true knowledge, and comprehend the mysteries of divine wisdom. Consider now, were the parched and barren soil of these hearts to remain unchanged, how could they ever become the Recipients of the revelation of the mysteries of God, and the Revealers of the divine Essence? Thus hath He said: "On the day when the earth shall be changed into another earth."[1]

[1 Qur'án 14:48.]

(Bahá'u'lláh, *The Kitáb-i-Íqán*, p. 45)

The heart must needs therefore be cleansed from the idle sayings of men, and sanctified from every earthly affection, so that it may discover the hidden meaning of divine inspiration, and become the treasury of the mysteries of divine knowledge.

(Bahá'u'lláh, *The Kitáb-i-Íqán*, p. 69)

The pure heart is one that is entirely cut away from self. To be selfless is to be pure.

('Abdu'l-Bahá, *'Abdu'l-Bahá in London*, p. 107)

O SON OF MAN! The temple of being is My throne; cleanse it of all things, that there I may be established and there I may abide.

(Bahá'u'lláh, *The Hidden Words*, Arabic #58)

O SON OF BEING! Thy heart is My home; sanctify it for My descent. Thy spirit is My place of revelation; cleanse it for My manifestation.

(Bahá'u'lláh, *The Hidden Words*, Arabic #59)

...if the mirror of his heart be already obscured by the dust of these learnings, he must needs cleanse and purify it ere the light of this mystery can be reflected therein.

(Bahá'u'lláh, *The Kitáb-i-Íqán*, p. 187)

…when a true seeker determineth to take the step of search in the path leading to the knowledge of the Ancient of Days, he must, before all else, cleanse and purify his heart, which is the seat of the revelation of the inner mysteries of God, from the obscuring dust of all acquired knowledge, and the allusions of the embodiments of satanic fancy. He must purge his breast, which is the sanctuary of the abiding love of the Beloved, of every defilement, and sanctify his soul from all that pertaineth to water and clay, from all shadowy and ephemeral attachments. He must so cleanse his heart that no remnant of either love or hate may linger therein, lest that love blindly incline him to error, or that hate repel him away from the truth.

(Bahá'u'lláh, *The Kitáb-i-Íqán*, p. 192)

When the channel of the human soul is cleansed of all worldly and impeding attachments, it will unfailingly perceive the breath of the Beloved across immeasurable distances, and will, led by its perfume, attain and enter the City of Certitude.

(Bahá'u'lláh, *The Kitáb-i-Íqán*, p. 195)

Wherefore must the veils of the satanic self be burned away at the fire of love, that the spirit may be purified and cleansed and thus may know the station of the Lord of the Worlds.

(Bahá'u'lláh, *The Seven Valleys*, p. 10)

O SON OF PASSION! Cleanse thyself from the defilement of riches and in perfect peace advance into the realm of poverty; that from the well-spring of detachment thou mayest quaff the wine of immortal life.

(Bahá'u'lláh, *The Hidden Words*, Persian #55)

Say: Rejoice not in the things ye possess; tonight they are yours, tomorrow others will possess them. Thus warneth you He Who is the All-Knowing, the All-Informed. Say: Can ye claim that what ye own is lasting or secure? Nay! By Myself, the All-Merciful, ye cannot, if ye be of them who judge fairly. The days of your life flee away as a breath of wind, and all your pomp and glory shall be folded up as were the pomp and glory of those gone before you. Reflect, O people! What hath become of your bygone days, your lost centuries? Happy the days that have been consecrated to the remembrance of God, and blessed the hours which have been spent in praise of Him Who is the All-Wise. By My life! Neither the pomp of the mighty, nor the wealth of the rich, nor even the ascendancy of the ungodly will endure. All will perish, at a word from Him. He, verily, is the All-Powerful, the All-Compelling, the Almighty. What advantage is there in the earthly things which men possess? That which shall profit them, they have utterly neglected. Erelong, they will awake from their slumber, and find themselves unable to obtain that which hath escaped them in the days of their Lord, the Almighty, the All-Praised. Did they but know it, they would renounce their all, that their names may be mentioned before His throne. They, verily, are accounted among the dead.

(Bahá'u'lláh, *The Kitáb-i-Aqdas*, p. 33)

Cast away that which ye possess, and, on the wings of detachment, soar beyond all created things. Thus biddeth you the Lord of creation, the movement of Whose Pen hath revolutionized the soul of mankind.

Know ye from what heights your Lord, the All-Glorious, is calling? Think ye that ye have recognized the Pen wherewith your Lord, the Lord of all names, commandeth you? Nay, by My life! Did ye but know it, ye would renounce the world, and would hasten with your whole hearts to the presence of the Well-Beloved. Your spirits would be so transported by His Word as to throw into commotion the Greater World -- how much more this small and petty one! Thus have the showers of My bounty been poured down from the heaven of My loving-kindness, as a token of My grace, that ye may be of the thankful.

(Bahá'u'lláh, *The Kitáb-i-Aqdas*, p. 39)

The essence of detachment is for man to turn his face towards the courts of the Lord, to enter His Presence, behold His Countenance, and stand as witness before Him.

(Bahá'u'lláh, *Tablets of Bahá'u'lláh*, p. 155)

He must purge his breast, which is the sanctuary of the abiding love of the Beloved, of every defilement, and sanctify his soul from all that pertaineth to water and clay, from all shadowy and ephemeral attachments.

(Bahá'u'lláh, *Gleanings from the Writings of Bahá'u'lláh*, p. 264)

I swear by the life of Him Who is the Desire of the world! Were a man to ponder in his heart he would, free of all attachment to the world, hasten unto the Most Great Light and would purge and purify himself from the dust of vain imaginings and the smoke of idle fancy. What could have prompted the people of the past to err and by whom were they misled? They still reject the truth and have turned towards their own selfish desires. This Wronged One calleth aloud for the sake of God. Whosoever wisheth, let him turn thereunto; whosoever wisheth, let him turn away. Verily God can well afford to dispense with all things, whether of the past or of the future.

(Bahá'u'lláh, *Tablets of Bahá'u'lláh*, p. 41)

Cast away the things current amongst men and take fast hold on that whereunto ye are bidden by virtue of the Will of the Ordainer, the Ancient of Days.

(Bahá'u'lláh, *Tablets of Bahá'u'lláh*, p. 78)

The friends of God have not, nor will they ever, set their hopes upon the world and its ephemeral possessions.
(Bahá'u'lláh, *The Summons of the Lord of Hosts*, p. 110)

Say: He is not to be numbered with the people of Bahá who followeth his mundane desires, or fixeth his heart on things of the earth. He is My true follower who, if he come to a valley of pure gold, will pass straight through it aloof as a cloud, and will neither turn back, nor pause. Such a man is, assuredly, of Me. From his garment the Concourse on high can inhale the fragrance of sanctity.... And if he met the fairest and most comely of women, he would not feel his heart seduced by the least shadow of desire for her beauty. Such an one, indeed, is the creation of spotless chastity. Thus instructeth you the Pen of the Ancient of Days, as bidden by your Lord, the Almighty, the All-Bountiful.
(Bahá'u'lláh, *Gleanings from the Writings of Bahá'u'lláh*, p. 118)

Blessed is the soul which, at the hour of its separation from the body, is sanctified from the vain imaginings of the peoples of the world. Such a soul liveth and moveth in accordance with the Will of its Creator, and entereth the all-highest Paradise.
(Bahá'u'lláh, *Gleanings from the Writings of Bahá'u'lláh*, p. 155)

Thou hast, moreover, asked Me concerning the state of the soul after its separation from the body. Know thou, of a truth, that if the soul of man hath walked in the ways of God, it will, assuredly, return and be gathered to the glory of the Beloved. By the righteousness of God! It shall attain a station such as no pen can depict, or tongue describe. The soul that hath remained faithful to the Cause of God, and stood unwaveringly firm in His Path shall, after his ascension, be possessed of such power that all the worlds which the Almighty hath created can benefit through him. Such a soul provideth, at the bidding of the Ideal King and Divine Educator, the pure leaven that leaveneth the world of being, and furnisheth the power through which the arts and wonders of the world are made manifest. Consider how meal needeth leaven to be leavened with. Those souls that are the symbols of detachment are the leaven of the world. Meditate on this, and be of the thankful.

(Bahá'u'lláh, *Gleanings from the Writings of Bahá'u'lláh*, p. 161)

For every one of you his paramount duty is to choose for himself that on which no other may infringe and none usurp from him. Such a thing -- and to this the Almighty is My witness -- is the love of God, could ye but perceive it.

(Bahá'u'lláh, *Gleanings from the Writings of Bahá'u'lláh*, p. 261)

Follow not, therefore, your earthly desires, and violate not the Covenant of God, nor break your pledge to Him. With firm determination, with the whole affection of your heart, and with the full force of your words, turn ye unto Him, and walk not in the ways of the foolish. The world is but a show, vain and empty, a mere nothing, bearing the semblance of reality. Set not your affections upon it. Break not the bond that uniteth you with your Creator, and be not of those that have erred and strayed from His ways. Verily I say, the world is like the vapor in a desert, which the thirsty dreameth to be water and striveth after it with all his might, until when he cometh unto it, he findeth it to be mere illusion. It may, moreover, be likened unto the lifeless image of the beloved whom the lover hath sought and found, in the end, after long search and to his utmost regret, to be such as cannot "fatten nor appease his hunger.

(Bahá'u'lláh, *Gleanings from the Writings of Bahá'u'lláh*, p. 327)

Ye are even as the bird which soareth, with the full force of its mighty wings and with complete and joyous confidence, through the immensity of the heavens, until, impelled to satisfy its hunger, it turneth longingly to the water and clay of the earth below it, and, having been entrapped in the mesh of its desire, findeth itself impotent to resume its flight to the realms whence it came. Powerless to shake off the burden weighing on its sullied wings, that bird, hitherto an inmate of the heavens, is now forced to seek a dwelling-place upon the dust. Wherefore, O My servants, defile not your wings with the clay of wayward-ness and vain desires, and suffer them not to be stained with the dust of envy and hate, that ye may not be hindered from soaring in the heavens of My divine knowledge.

(Bahá'u'lláh, *Gleanings from the Writings of Bahá'u'lláh*, p. 325)

O SON OF BEING! If thine heart be set upon this eternal, imperishable dominion, and this ancient, everlasting life, forsake this mortal and fleeting sovereignty.

(Bahá'u'lláh, *The Hidden Words*, Arabic #54)

O SON OF MAN! The temple of being is My throne; cleanse it of all things, that there I may be established and there I may abide.

(Bahá'u'lláh, *The Hidden Words*, Arabic #58)

O SON OF BEING! Thy heart is My home; sanctify it for My descent. Thy spirit is My place of revelation; cleanse it for My manifestation.

(Bahá'u'lláh, *The Hidden Words*, Arabic #59)

O YE SONS OF SPIRIT! Ye are My treasury, for in you I have treasured the pearls of My mysteries and the gems of My knowledge. Guard them from the strangers amidst My servants and from the ungodly amongst My people.

(Bahá'u'lláh, *The Hidden Words*, Arabic #69)

Wert thou to attain to but a dewdrop of the crystal waters of divine knowledge, thou wouldst readily realize that true life is not the life of the flesh but the life of the spirit.

(Bahá'u'lláh, *The Kitáb-i-Íqán*, p. 120)

By 'riches' therefore is meant independence of all else but God, and by 'poverty' the lack of things that are of God.

(Bahá'u'lláh, *The Kitáb-i-Íqán*, p. 132)

The essence of wealth is love for Me; whoso loveth Me is the possessor of all things, and he that loveth Me not is indeed of the poor and needy. This is that which the Finger of Glory and Splendour hath revealed.

(Bahá'u'lláh, *Tablets of Bahá'u'lláh*, p. 156)

He who attaineth to My love hath title to a throne of gold, to sit thereon in honour over all the world; he who is deprived thereof, though he sit upon the dust, that dust would seek refuge with God, the Lord of all Religions.

(Bahá'u'lláh, *The Kitáb-i-Aqdas*, p. 32)

Blessed are they that have soared on the wings of detachment and attained the station which, as ordained by God, overshadoweth the entire creation, whom neither the vain imaginations of the learned, nor the multitude of the hosts of the earth have succeeded in deflecting from His Cause. Who is there among you, O people, who will renounce the world, and draw nigh unto God, the Lord of all names? Where is he to be found who, through the power of My name that transcendeth all created things, will cast away the things that men possess, and cling, with all his might, to the things which God, the Knower of the unseen and of the seen, hath bidden him observe? Thus hath His bounty been sent down unto men, His testimony fulfilled, and His proof shone forth above the Horizon of mercy. Rich is the prize that shall be won by him who hath believed and exclaimed: "Lauded art Thou, O Beloved of all worlds! Magnified be Thy name, O Thou the Desire of every understanding heart!"

(Bahá'u'lláh, *Gleanings from the Writings of Bahá'u'lláh*, p. 34)

It behoveth the people of Bahá to die to the world and all that is therein, to be so detached from all earthly things that the inmates of Paradise may inhale from their garment the sweet smelling savor of sanctity, that all the peoples of the earth may recognize in their faces the brightness of the All-Merciful, and that through them may be spread abroad the signs and tokens of God, the Almighty, the All-Wise. They that have tarnished the fair name of the Cause of God, by following the things of the flesh -- these are in palpable error!

(Bahá'u'lláh, *Gleanings from the Writings of Bahá'u'lláh*, p. 100)

O SON OF GLORY! Be swift in the path of holiness, and enter the heaven of communion with Me. Cleanse thy heart with the burnish of the spirit, and hasten to the court of the Most High.

(Bahá'u'lláh, *The Hidden Words*, Persian #8)

O SON OF DUST! Blind thine eyes, that thou mayest behold My beauty; stop thine ears, that thou mayest hearken unto the sweet melody of My voice; empty thyself of all learning, that thou mayest partake of My knowledge; and sanctify thyself from riches, that thou mayest obtain a lasting share from the ocean of My eternal wealth. Blind thine eyes, that is, to all save My beauty; stop thine ears to all save My word; empty thyself of all learning save the knowledge of Me; that with a

clear vision, a pure heart and an attentive ear thou mayest enter
the court of My holiness.

(Bahá'u'lláh, The Hidden Words, Persian #11)

O MY SERVANT! Free thyself from the fetters of this
world, and loose thy soul from the prison of self. Seize thy
chance, for it will come to thee no more.

(Bahá'u'lláh, The Hidden Words, Persian #40)

O CHILDREN OF ADAM! Holy words and pure and
goodly deeds ascend unto the heaven of celestial glory. Strive
that your deeds may be cleansed from the dust of self and
hypocrisy and find favor at the court of glory; for ere long the
assayers of mankind shall, in the holy presence of the Adored
One, accept naught but absolute virtue and deeds of stainless
purity. This is the daystar of wisdom and of divine mystery that
hath shone above the horizon of the divine will. Blessed are
they that turn thereunto.

(Bahá'u'lláh, The Hidden Words, Persian #69)

O MY FRIEND! Thou art the daystar of the heavens of
My holiness, let not the defilement of the world eclipse thy
splendor. Rend asunder the veil of heedlessness, that from behind the clouds thou mayest emerge resplendent and array all
things with the apparel of life.

(Bahá'u'lláh, The Hidden Words, Persian #73)

It is incumbent upon thee, and upon the followers of Him
Who is the Eternal Truth, to summon all men to whatsoever
shall sanctify them from all attachment to the things of the
earth and purge them from its defilements, that the sweet smell
of the raiment of the All-Glorious may be smelled from all
them that love Him.

(Bahá'u'lláh, Gleanings from the Writings of Bahá'u'lláh, p. 201)

O SON OF MY HANDMAID! Didst thou behold immortal sovereignty, thou wouldst strive to pass from this fleeting world. But to conceal the one from thee and to reveal the other is a mystery which none but the pure in heart can comprehend.

(Bahá'u'lláh, *The Hidden Words*, Persian #41)

As to Paradise: It is a reality and there can be no doubt about it, and now in this world it is realized through love of Me and My good-pleasure. Whosoever attaineth unto it God will aid him in this world below, and after death He will enable him to gain admittance into Paradise whose vastness is as that of heaven and earth. Therein the Maids of glory and holiness will wait upon him in the daytime and in the night season, while the day-star of the unfading beauty of his Lord will at all times shed its radiance upon him and he will shine so brightly that no one shall bear to gaze at him. Such is the dispensation of Providence, yet the people are shut out by a grievous veil. Likewise apprehend thou the nature of hell-fire and be of them that truly believe. For every act performed there shall be a recompense according to the estimate of God, and unto this the very ordinances and prohibitions prescribed by the Almighty amply bear witness. For surely if deeds were not rewarded and yielded no fruit, then the Cause of God -- exalted is He -- would prove futile. Immeasurably high is He exalted above such blasphemies! However, unto them that are rid of all attachments a deed is, verily, its own reward. Were We to enlarge upon this theme numerous Tablets would need to be written.

(Bahá'u'lláh, *Tablets of Bahá'u'lláh*, p. 188 189)

He, verily, hath willed for you that which is yet beyond your knowledge, but which shall be known to you when, after this fleeting life, your souls soar heavenwards and the trappings of your earthly joys are folded up.

(Bahá'u'lláh, *The Kitáb-i-Aqdas*, p. 55)

The fleeting hours of man's life on earth pass swiftly by and the little that still remaineth shall come to an end, but that which endureth and lasteth for evermore is the fruit that man reapeth from his servitude at the Divine Threshold.

('Abdu'l-Bahá, *Selections from the Writings of 'Abdu'l-Bahá*, p. 233)

He should cleanse his heart from all evil passions and corrupt desires, for the fear of God is the weapon that can render him victorious, the primary instrument whereby he can achieve his purpose. The fear of God is the shield that defendeth His Cause, the buckler that enableth His people to attain to victory. It is a standard that no man can abase, a force that no power can rival. By its aid, and by the leave of Him Who is the Lord of Hosts, they that have drawn nigh unto God have been able to subdue and conquer the citadels of the hearts of men.

(Bahá'u'lláh, *Gleanings from the Writings of Bahá'u'lláh*, p. 272)

O SON OF BEING! Bring thyself to account each day ere thou art summoned to a reckoning; for death, unheralded, shall come upon thee and thou shalt be called to give account for thy deeds.

(Bahá'u'lláh, *The Hidden Words*, Arabic #31)

'THEY ARE COMMISSIONED TO
USE THE INSPIRATION
OF THEIR WORDS'

Led by the light of unfailing guidance, and invested with supreme sovereignty, They are commissioned to use the inspiration of Their words, the effusions of Their infallible grace and the sanctifying breeze of Their Revelation for the cleansing of every longing heart and receptive spirit from the dross and dust of earthly cares and limitations. Then, and only then, will the Trust of God, latent in the reality of man, emerge, as resplendent as the rising Orb of Divine Revelation, from behind the veil of concealment, and implant the ensign of its revealed glory upon the summits of men's hearts.

(Bahá'u'lláh, *Gleanings from the Writings of Bahá'u'lláh*, p. 67)

In like manner, endeavour to comprehend the meaning of the "changing of the earth." Know thou, that upon whatever hearts the bountiful showers of mercy, raining from the "heaven" of divine Revelation, have fallen, the earth of those hearts hath verily been changed into the earth of divine knowledge and wisdom.

(Bahá'u'lláh, *The Kitáb-i-Íqán*, p. 45)

God's purpose in sending His Prophets unto men is twofold. The first is to liberate the children of men from the darkness of ignorance, and guide them to the light of true understanding. The second is to ensure the peace and tranquillity of mankind, and provide all the means by which they can be established.

(Bahá'u'lláh, *Gleanings from the Writings of Bahá'u'lláh*, p. 79)

All praise and glory be to God Who, through the power of His might, hath delivered His creation from the nakedness of non-existence, and clothed it with the mantle of life. From among all created things He hath singled out for His special favor the pure, the gem-like reality of man, and invested it with

a unique capacity of knowing Him and of reflecting the great-
ness of His glory. This twofold distinction conferred upon him
hath cleansed away from his heart the rust of every vain desire,
and made him worthy of the vesture with which his Creator
hath deigned to clothe him. It hath served to rescue his soul
from the wretchedness of ignorance.

This robe with which the body and soul of man hath been
adorned is the very foundation of his well-being and develop-
ment. Oh, how blessed the day when, aided by the grace and
might of the one true God, man will have freed himself from
the bondage and corruption of the world and all that is therein,
and will have attained unto true and abiding rest beneath the
shadow of the Tree of Knowledge!

(Bahá'u'lláh, *Gleanings from the Writings of Bahá'u'lláh*, p. 77)

Say: God hath made My hidden love the key to the Treasure; would that ye might perceive it! But for the key, the Treasure would to all eternity have remained concealed; would that
ye might believe it! Say: This is the Source of Revelation, the
Dawning-place of Splendour, Whose brightness hath illumined
the horizons of the world. Would that ye might understand!
This is, verily, that fixed Decree through which every irrevo-
cable decree hath been established.

(Bahá'u'lláh, *The Kitáb-i-Aqdas*, p. 24)

In this day, they that are submerged beneath the ocean of
ancient Knowledge, and dwell within the ark of divine wisdom,
forbid the people such idle pursuits. Their shining breasts are,
praise be to God, sanctified from every trace of such learning,
and are exalted above such grievous veils. We have consumed
this densest of all veils, with the fire of the love of the Beloved
-- the veil referred to in the saying: "The most grievous of all
veils is the veil of knowledge." Upon its ashes, We have reared

the tabernacle of divine knowledge. We have, praise be to God, burned the "veils of glory" with the fire of the beauty of the Best-Beloved. We have driven from the human heart all else but Him Who is the Desire of the world, and glory therein. We cleave to no knowledge but His Knowledge, and set our hearts on naught save the effulgent glories of His light.

(Bahá'u'lláh, *The Kitáb-i-Íqán*, p. 187)

For were men to abide by and observe the divine teachings, every trace of evil would be banished from the face of the earth.

(Bahá'u'lláh, *Tablets of Bahá'u'lláh*, p. 176)

Were any man to ponder in his heart that which the Pen of the Most High hath revealed and to taste of its sweetness, he would, of a certainty, find himself emptied and delivered from his own desires, and utterly subservient to the Will of the Almighty. Happy is the man that hath attained so high a station, and hath not deprived himself of so bountiful a grace.

(Bahá'u'lláh, *Gleanings from the Writings of Bahá'u'lláh*, p. 342)

O SON OF MAN! The light hath shone on thee from the horizon of the sacred Mount and the spirit of enlightenment hath breathed in the Sinai of thy heart. Wherefore, free thyself from the veils of idle fancies and enter into My court, that thou mayest be fit for everlasting life and worthy to meet Me. Thus may death not come upon thee, neither weariness nor trouble.

(Bahá'u'lláh, *The Hidden Words*, Arabic #63)

Hearken thou unto the Words of thy Lord and purify thy heart from every illusion so that the effulgent light of the remembrance of thy Lord may shed its radiance upon it, and it may attain the station of certitude.

(Bahá'u'lláh, *Tablets of Bahá'u'lláh*, p. 182 183)

...cleanse thyself with the waters of detachment that have flowed out from the Supreme Pen...

(Bahá'u'lláh, *Epistle to the Son of the Wolf*, p. 11)

Verily I say: Incline your ears to My sweet voice, and sanctify yourselves from the defilement of your evil passions and corrupt desires. They who dwell within the tabernacle of God, and are established upon the seats of everlasting glory, will refuse, though they be dying of hunger, to stretch their hands and seize unlawfully the property of their neighbor, however vile and worthless he may be.

(Bahá'u'lláh, *Gleanings from the Writings of Bahá'u'lláh*, p. 298)

A Book sent down in truth unto men of insight! It biddeth the people to observe justice and to work righteousness, and forbiddeth them to follow their corrupt inclinations and carnal desires, if perchance the children of men might be roused from their slumber.

Say: Follow, O people, what hath been prescribed unto you in Our Tablets, and walk not after the imaginations which the sowers of mischief have devised, they that commit wickedness and impute it to God, the Most Holy, the All-Glorious, the Most Exalted. Say: We have accepted to be tried by ills and troubles, that ye may sanctify yourselves from all earthly defilements. Why, then, refuse ye to ponder Our purpose in your hearts? By the righteousness of God! Whoso will reflect upon the tribulations We have suffered, his soul will assuredly melt away with sorrow. Thy Lord Himself beareth witness to the truth of My words. We have sustained the weight of all calamities to sanctify you from all earthly corruption, and ye are yet indifferent.

Say: It behoveth every one that holdeth fast to the hem of Our Robe to be untainted by anything from which the Concourse on high may be averse. Thus hath it been decreed by thy Lord, the All-Glorious, in this His perspicuous Tablet. Say: Set ye aside My love, and commit what grieveth Mine heart? What is it that hindereth you from comprehending what hath been revealed unto you by Him Who is the All-Knowing, the All-Wise?

(Bahá'u'lláh, *Gleanings from the Writings of Bahá'u'lláh*, p. 305)

Whatever, therefore, He saith unto you is wholly for the sake of God, that haply the peoples of the earth may cleanse their hearts from the stain of evil desire, may rend its veil asunder, and attain unto the knowledge of the one true God -- the most exalted station to which any man can aspire.

(Bahá'u'lláh, *Gleanings from the Writings of Bahá'u'lláh*, p. 84)

Whoso followeth his Lord, will renounce the world and all that is therein

(Bahá'u'lláh, *Gleanings from the Writings of Bahá'u'lláh*, p. 211)

O MY FRIENDS! Have ye forgotten that true and radiant morn, when in those hallowed and blessed surroundings ye were all gathered in My presence beneath the shade of the tree of life, which is planted in the all-glorious paradise? Awe-struck ye listened as I gave utterance to these three most holy words: O friends! Prefer not your will to Mine, never desire that which I have not desired for you, and approach Me not with lifeless hearts, defiled with worldly desires and cravings. Would ye but sanctify your souls, ye would at this present hour recall that place and those surroundings, and the truth of My utterance should be made evident unto all of you.

(Bahá'u'lláh, *The Hidden Words*, Persian #19)

O CHILDREN OF DESIRE! Put away the garment of vainglory, and divest yourselves of the attire of haughtiness. In the third of the most holy lines writ and recorded in the Ruby Tablet by the pen of the unseen this is revealed:

O BRETHREN! Be forbearing one with another and set not your affections on things below. Pride not yourselves in your glory, and be not ashamed of abasement. By My beauty! I have created all things from dust, and to dust will I return them again.

(Bahá'u'lláh, *The Hidden Words*, Persian #47 and #48)

Say: O people! The Lamp of God is burning; take heed, lest the fierce winds of your disobedience extinguish its light. Now is the time to arise and magnify the Lord, your God. Strive not after bodily comforts, and keep your heart pure and stainless. The Evil One is lying in wait, ready to entrap you. Gird yourselves against his wicked devices, and, led by the light of the name of the one true God, deliver yourselves from the darkness that surroundeth you.

(Bahá'u'lláh, *Gleanings from the Writings of Bahá'u'lláh*, p. 167)

Cast away, in My name that transcendeth all other names, the things ye possess, and immerse yourselves in this Ocean in whose depths lay hidden the pearls of wisdom and of utterance, an ocean that surgeth in My name, the All-Merciful. Thus instructeth you He with Whom is the Mother Book.

(Bahá'u'lláh, *Gleanings from the Writings of Bahá'u'lláh*, p. 33)

As to him who turneth aside, and swelleth with pride, after that the clear tokens have come unto him, from the Revealer of signs, his work shall God bring to naught. He, in truth, hath power over all things. Man's actions are acceptable after his having recognized (the Manifestation). He that turneth aside from the True One is indeed the most veiled amongst His creatures. Thus hath it been decreed by Him Who is the Almighty, the Most Powerful.

(Bahá'u'lláh, *Epistle to the Son of the Wolf*, p. 60)

O peoples of the earth! Incline your inner ears to the call of this Wronged One and pause to reflect upon the story that We have recounted. Perchance ye may not be consumed by the fire of self and passion, nor allow the vain and worthless objects of this nether world to withhold you from Him Who is the Eternal Truth. Glory and abasement, riches and poverty, tranquility and tribulation, all will pass away, and all the peoples of the earth will erelong be laid to rest in their tombs. It behoveth therefore every man of insight to fix his gaze upon the goal of eternity, that perchance by the grace of Him Who is the Ancient King he may attain unto the immortal Kingdom and abide beneath the shade of the Tree of His Revelation.

(Bahá'u'lláh, *The Summons of the Lord of Hosts*, p. 169)

O SON OF MAN! Wert thou to speed through the immensity of space and traverse the expanse of heaven, yet thou wouldst find no rest save in submission to Our command and humbleness before Our Face.

(Bahá'u'lláh, *The Hidden Words*, Arabic #40)

God is Our witness! Whoever hath tasted the sweetness of those words will never consent to transgress the bounds which God hath fixed, neither will he turn his gaze towards any one except his Well-Beloved. Such a man will, with his inner eye, readily recognize how altogether vain and fleeting are the things of this world, and will set his affections on things above.

(Bahá'u'lláh, *Gleanings from the Writings of Bahá'u'lláh*, p. 298)

O MY BROTHER! Hearken to the delightsome words of My honeyed tongue, and quaff the stream of mystic holiness from My sugar-shedding lips. Sow the seeds of My divine wisdom in the pure soil of thy heart, and water them with the water of certitude, that the hyacinths of My knowledge and wisdom may spring up fresh and green in the sacred city of thy heart.

(Bahá'u'lláh, *The Hidden Words*, Persian #33)

We enjoin the servants of God and His handmaidens to be pure and to fear God, that they may shake off the slumber of their corrupt desires, and turn toward God, the Maker of the heavens and of the earth.

(Bahá'u'lláh, *Epistle to the Son of the Wolf*, p. 22)

O ye loved ones of God! In this, the Bahá'í dispensation, God's Cause is spirit unalloyed. His Cause belongeth not to the material world. It cometh neither for strife nor war, nor for acts of mischief or of shame; it is neither for quarrelling with other Faiths, nor for conflicts with the nations. Its only army is the love of God, its only joy the clear wine of His knowledge, its only battle the expounding of the Truth; its one crusade is against the insistent self, the evil promptings of the human heart. Its victory is to submit and yield, and to be selfless is its everlasting glory.

('Abdu'l-Bahá, *Selections from the Writings of 'Abdu'l-Bahá*, p. 256)

O people of the world! Follow not the promptings of the self, for it summoneth insistently to wickedness and lust; follow, rather, Him Who is the Possessor of all created things, Who biddeth you to show forth piety, and manifest the fear of God.

(Bahá'u'lláh, *The Kitáb-i-Aqdas*, p. 41)

O banished and faithful friend! Quench the thirst of heedlessness with the sanctified waters of My grace, and chase the gloom of remoteness through the morning-light of My Divine presence. Suffer not the habitation wherein dwelleth My undying love for thee to be destroyed through the tyranny of covetous desires, and overcloud not the beauty of the heavenly Youth with the dust of self and passion. Clothe thyself with the essence of righteousness, and let thine heart be afraid of none except God. Obstruct not the luminous spring of thy soul with the thorns and brambles of vain and inordinate affections, and impede not the flow of the living waters that stream from the fountain of thine heart. Set all thy hope in God, and cleave tenaciously to His unfailing mercy. Who else but Him can enrich the destitute, and deliver the fallen from his abasement?

O My servants! Were ye to discover the hidden, the shoreless oceans of My incorruptible wealth, ye would, of a certainty, esteem as nothing the world, nay, the entire creation. Let the flame of search burn with such fierceness within your hearts as to enable you to attain your supreme and most exalted goal -- the station at which ye can draw nigh unto, and be united with, your Best-Beloved....

O My servants! Let not your vain hopes and idle fancies sap the foundations of your belief in the All-Glorious God, inasmuch as such imaginings have been wholly unprofitable unto men, and failed to direct their steps unto the straight Path.

(Bahá'u'lláh, *Gleanings from the Writings of Bahá'u'lláh*, p. 322)

O wayfarer in the path of God! Take thou thy portion of the ocean of His grace, and deprive not thyself of the things that lie hidden in its depths. Be thou of them that have partaken of its treasures. A dewdrop out of this ocean would, if shed upon all that are in the heavens and on the earth, suffice to enrich them with the bounty of God, the Almighty, the All-Knowing, the All-Wise. With the hands of renunciation draw forth from its life-giving waters, and sprinkle therewith all created things, that they may be cleansed from all man-made limitations and may approach the mighty seat of God, this hallowed and resplendent Spot.

(Bahá'u'lláh, *Gleanings from the Writings of Bahá'u'lláh*, p. 279)

O SON OF WORLDLINESS! Pleasant is the realm of being, wert thou to attain thereto; glorious is the domain of eternity, shouldst thou pass beyond the world of mortality; sweet is the holy ecstasy if thou drinkest of the mystic chalice from the hands of the celestial Youth. Shouldst thou attain this station, thou wouldst be freed from destruction and death, from toil and sin.

(Bahá'u'lláh, *The Hidden Words*, Persian #70)

Praised be Thou, O Lord my God! This is Thy servant who hath quaffed from the hands of Thy grace the wine of Thy tender mercy, and tasted of the savor of Thy love in Thy days. I beseech Thee, by the embodiments of Thy names whom no grief can hinder from rejoicing in Thy love or from gazing on Thy face, and whom all the hosts of the heedless are powerless to cause to turn aside from the path of Thy pleasure, to supply him with the good things Thou dost possess, and to raise him up to such heights that he will regard the world even as a shadow that vanisheth swifter than the twinkling of an eye.

Keep him safe also, O my God, by the power of Thine immeasurable majesty, from all that Thou abhorrest. Thou art, verily, his Lord and the Lord of all worlds.

(Bahá'u'lláh, *Prayers and Meditations by Bahá'u'lláh*, p. 15)

"'The Master Key' to Self-Mastery is Self-Forgetting"

Today the confirmations of the Kingdom of Abhá are with those who renounce themselves, forget their own opinions, cast aside personalities and are thinking of the welfare of others.... Whosoever is occupied with himself is wandering in the desert of heedlessness and regret. The 'Master Key' to self-mastery is self- forgetting. The road to the palace of life is through the path of renunciation.

('Abdu'l-Bahá, *Star of the West*, Vol. XVII, p. 348)
(*Lights of Guidance*, p. 114)

Hence, one of the Prophets of God hath asked: "O my Lord, how shall we reach unto Thee?" And the answer came, "Leave thyself behind, and then approach Me."

(Bahá'u'lláh, *The Four Valleys*, p. 55)

Turn your faces away from the contemplation of your own finite selves and fix your eyes upon the Everlasting Radiance; then will your souls receive in full measure the Divine Power of the Spirit and the Blessings of the Infinite Bounty.

('Abdu'l-Bahá, *Paris Talks*, p. 166)

In one of His meditations, Bahá'u'lláh entreats God to supply the believers with "the choice Wine of Thy mercy, that it may cause them to be forgetful of any one except Thee, and to arise to serve Thy Cause, and to be steadfast in their love for Thee".

(Bahá'u'lláh, *The Kitáb-i-Aqdas*, p. 166)

Center your thoughts in the Well-Beloved, rather than in your own selves.

(Bahá'u'lláh, *Gleanings from the Writings of Bahá'u'lláh*, p. 167)

O SON OF DESIRE! Give ear unto this: Never shall mortal eye recognize the everlasting Beauty, nor the lifeless heart delight in aught but in the withered bloom. For like seeketh like, and taketh pleasure in the company of its kind.

(Bahá'u'lláh, *The Hidden Words*, Persian #10)

O MAN OF TWO VISIONS! Close one eye and open the other. Close one to the world and all that is therein, and open the other to the hallowed beauty of the Beloved.

(Bahá'u'lláh, *The Hidden Words*, Persian #12)

O SON OF DUST! All that is in heaven and earth I have ordained for thee, except the human heart, which I have made the habitation of My beauty and glory; yet thou didst give My home and dwelling to another than Me; and whenever the manifestation of My holiness sought His own abode, a stranger found He there, and, homeless, hastened unto the sanctuary of the Beloved. Notwithstanding I have concealed thy secret and desired not thy shame.

(Bahá'u'lláh, *The Hidden Words*, Persian #27)

O SON OF SPIRIT! Burst thy cage asunder, and even as the phoenix of love soar into the firmament of holiness. Renounce thyself and, filled with the spirit of mercy, abide in the realm of celestial sanctity.

(Bahá'u'lláh, *The Hidden Words*, Persian #38)

O MY SERVANT! Thou art even as a finely tempered sword concealed in the darkness of its sheath and its value hidden from the artificer's knowledge. Wherefore come forth from the sheath of self and desire that thy worth may be made resplendent and manifest unto all the world.

(Bahá'u'lláh, *The Hidden Words*, Persian #72)

Their hearts seem not to be inclined to knowledge and the door thereof, neither think they of its manifestations, inasmuch as in idle fancy they have found the door that leadeth unto earthly riches, whereas in the manifestation of the Revealer of knowledge they find naught but the call to self-sacrifice.

(Bahá'u'lláh, *The Kitáb-i-Íqán*, p. 29)

Thine eye is My trust, suffer not the dust of vain desires to becloud its luster. Thine ear is a sign of My bounty, let not the tumult of unseemly motives turn it away from My Word that encompasseth all creation. Thine heart is My treasury, allow not the treacherous hand of self to rob thee of the pearls which I have treasured therein. Thine hand is a symbol of My loving-kindness, hinder it not from holding fast unto My guarded and hidden Tablets.... Unasked, I have showered upon thee My grace. Unpetitioned, I have fulfilled thy wish. In spite of thy undeserving, I have singled thee out for My richest, My incalculable favors.... O My servants! Be as resigned and submissive as the earth, that from the soil of your being there may blossom the fragrant, the holy and multicolored hyacinths of My knowledge. Be ablaze as the fire, that ye may burn away the veils of heedlessness and set aglow, through the quickening energies of the love of God, the chilled and wayward heart. Be light and untrammeled as the breeze, that ye may obtain admittance into the precincts of My court, My inviolable Sanctuary.

(Bahá'u'lláh, *Gleanings from the Writings of Bahá'u'lláh*, p. 320)

O my brother! A divine Mine only can yield the gems of divine knowledge, and the fragrance of the mystic Flower can be inhaled only in the ideal Garden, and the lilies of ancient wisdom can blossom nowhere except in the city of a stainless heart. "In a rich soil, its plants spring forth abundantly by permission of its Lord, and in that soil which is bad, they spring forth but scantily." [3]

[3 Qur'án 7:57.]
(Bahá'u'lláh, *The Kitáb-i-Íqán*, p. 191)

"... As soon as one feels a little better than, a little superior to, the rest, he is in a dangerous position, and unless he casts away the seed of such an evil thought, he is not a fit instrument for the service of the Kingdom. Dissatisfaction with oneself is a sign of progress. The soul who is satisfied with himself is the manifestation of Satan, and the one who is not contented with himself is the manifestation of the Merciful. If a person has a thousand good qualities he must not look at them; nay, rather he must strive to find out his own defects and imperfections. ...However much a man may progress, yet he is imperfect, because there is always a point ahead of him. No sooner does he look up towards that point than he become dissatisfied with his own condition, and aspires to attain to that. Praising one's own self is the sign of selfishness."
-- Diary of Mirza Ahmad Sohrab, 1914.

('Abdu'l-Bahá in J.E. Esslemont, *Bahá'u'lláh and the New Era*, p. 83)

Charity is pleasing and praiseworthy in the sight of God and is regarded as a prince among goodly deeds. Consider ye and call to mind that which the All-Merciful hath revealed in the Qur'án: "They prefer them before themselves, though poverty be their own lot. And with such as are preserved from their own covetousness shall it be well." [1] Viewed in this light, the blessed utterance above is, in truth, the day-star of utterances. Blessed is he who preferreth his brother before himself. Verily, such a man is reckoned, by virtue of the Will of God, the All-Knowing, the All-Wise, with the people of Bahá who dwell in the Crimson Ark.

[1 Qur'án 59:9.]
(Bahá'u'lláh, *Tablets of Bahá'u'lláh*, p. 71)

They who are possessed of riches, however, must have the utmost regard for the poor, for great is the honor destined by God for those poor who are steadfast in patience. By My life! There is no honor, except what God may please to bestow, that can compare to this honor. Great is the blessedness awaiting the poor that endure patiently and conceal their sufferings, and well is it with the rich who bestow their riches on the needy and prefer them before themselves.

Please God, the poor may exert themselves and strive to earn the means of livelihood. This is a duty which, in this most great Revelation, hath been prescribed unto every one, and is accounted in the sight of God as a goodly deed. Whoso observeth this duty, the help of the invisible One shall most certainly aid him. He can enrich, through His grace, whomsoever He pleaseth. He, verily, hath power over all things....

Tell, O 'Alí, the loved ones of God that equity is the most fundamental among human virtues. The evaluation of all things must needs depend upon it.

(Bahá'u'lláh, *Gleanings from the Writings of Bahá'u'lláh,* p. 201)

Until a being setteth his foot in the plane of sacrifice, he is bereft of every favour and grace; and this plane of sacrifice is the realm of dying to the self, that the radiance of the living God may then shine forth. The martyr's field is the place of detachment from self, that the anthems of eternity may be upraised. Do all ye can to become wholly weary of self, and bind yourselves to that Countenance of Splendours; and once ye have reached such heights of servitude, ye will find, gathered within your shadow, all created things. This is boundless grace; this is the highest sovereignty; this is the life that dieth not. All else save this is at the last but manifest perdition and great loss.

('Abdu'l-Bahá, *Selections from the Writings of 'Abdu'l-Bahá,* p. 76)

To attain eternal happiness one must suffer. He who has reached the state of self-sacrifice has true joy. Temporal joy will vanish.

('Abdu'l-Bahá, *Paris Talks,* p. 179)

That one indeed is a man who, today, dedicateth himself to the service of the entire human race. The Great Being saith: Blessed and happy is he that ariseth to promote the best interests of the peoples and kindreds of the earth.

(Bahá'u'lláh, *Gleanings from the Writings of Bahá'u'lláh,* p. 248)

These shall labour ceaselessly, by day and by night, shall heed neither trials nor woe, shall suffer no respite in their efforts, shall seek no repose, shall disregard all ease and comfort, and, detached and unsullied, shall consecrate every fleeting moment of their lives to the diffusion of the divine fragrance and the exaltation of God's holy Word.

('Abdu'l-Bahá, *Selections from the Writings of 'Abdu'l-Bahá,* p. 251)

Occupy thyself, during these fleeting days of thy life, with such deeds as will diffuse the fragrance of Divine good pleasure, and will be adorned with the ornament of His acceptance.

(Bahá'u'lláh, *Epistle to the Son of the Wolf,* p. 76)

Offer up, O people of Bahá, your substance, nay your very lives, for his assistance.

(Bahá'u'lláh, *Gleanings from the Writings of Bahá'u'lláh,* p. 211)

'Remembrance of Me Cleanseth All Things from Defilement '

Remembrance of Me cleanseth all things from defilement, could ye but perceive it.

(Bahá'u'lláh, *Gleanings from the Writings of Bahá'u'lláh*, p. 294)

True remembrance is to make mention of the Lord, the All-Praised, and forget aught else beside Him.

(Bahá'u'lláh, *Tablets of Bahá'u'lláh*, p. 155)

O SON OF EARTH! Wouldst thou have Me, seek none other than Me; and wouldst thou gaze upon My beauty, close thine eyes to the world and all that is therein; for My will and the will of another than Me, even as fire and water, cannot dwell together in one heart.

(Bahá'u'lláh, *The Hidden Words*, Persian #31)

O BEFRIENDED STRANGER! The candle of thine heart is lighted by the hand of My power, quench it not with the contrary winds of self and passion. The healer of all thine ills is remembrance of Me, forget it not. Make My love thy treasure and cherish it even as thy very sight and life.

(Bahá'u'lláh, *The Hidden Words*, Persian #32)

O SON OF SPIRIT! I created thee rich, why dost thou bring thyself down to poverty? Noble I made thee, wherewith dost thou abase thyself? Out of the essence of knowledge I gave thee being, why seekest thou enlightenment from anyone beside Me? Out of the clay of love I molded thee, how dost thou busy thyself with another? Turn thy sight unto thyself, that thou mayest find Me standing within thee, mighty, powerful and self-subsisting.

(Bahá'u'lláh, *The Hidden Words*, Arabic #13)

O SON OF UTTERANCE! Turn thy face unto Mine and renounce all save Me; for My sovereignty endureth and My dominion perisheth not. If thou seekest another than Me, yea, if thou searchest the universe for evermore, thy quest will be in vain.

(Bahá'u'lláh, *The Hidden Words*, Arabic #15)

O SON OF LIGHT! Forget all save Me and commune with My spirit. This is of the essence of My command, therefore turn unto it.

(Bahá'u'lláh, *The Hidden Words*, Arabic #16)

O SON OF MAN! Be thou content with Me and seek no other helper. For none but Me can ever suffice thee.

(Bahá'u'lláh, *The Hidden Words*, Arabic #17)

Meditate on what the poet hath written: "Wonder not, if my Best-Beloved be closer to me than mine own self; wonder at this, that I, despite such nearness, should still be so far from Him."... Considering what God hath revealed, that "We are closer to man than his life-vein," the poet hath, in allusion to this verse, stated that, though the revelation of my Best-Beloved hath so permeated my being that He is closer to me than my life-vein, yet, notwithstanding my certitude of its reality and my recognition of my station, I am still so far removed from Him. By this he meaneth that his heart, which is the seat of the All-Merciful and the throne wherein abideth the splendor of His revelation, is forgetful of its Creator, hath strayed from His path, hath shut out itself from His glory, and is stained with the defilement of earthly desires.

(Bahá'u'lláh, *Gleanings from the Writings of Bahá'u'lláh*, p. 184)

It is the waywardness of the heart that removeth it far from God, and condemneth it to remoteness from Him. Those hearts, however, that are aware of His Presence, are close to Him, and are to be regarded as having drawn nigh unto His throne.

(Bahá'u'lláh, *Gleanings from the Writings of Bahá'u'lláh*, p. 184)

Again He saith: "And also in your own selves: will ye not, then, behold the signs of God?" And yet again He revealeth: "And be ye not like those who forget God, and whom He hath therefore caused to forget their own selves." In this connection, He Who is the eternal King -- may the souls of all that dwell within the mystic Tabernacle be a sacrifice unto Him -- hath spoken: "He hath known God who hath known himself."

(Bahá'u'lláh, *Gleanings from the Writings of Bahá'u'lláh*, p. 176)

O My servants! Could ye apprehend with what wonders of My munificence and bounty I have willed to entrust your souls, ye would, of a truth, rid yourselves of attachment to all created things, and would gain a true knowledge of your own selves -- a knowledge which is the same as the comprehension of Mine own Being. Ye would find yourselves independent of all else but Me, and would perceive, with your inner and outer eye, and as manifest as the revelation of My effulgent Name, the seas of My loving-kindness and bounty moving within you. Suffer not your idle fancies, your evil passions, your insincerity and blindness of heart to dim the luster, or stain the sanctity, of so lofty a station.

(Bahá'u'lláh, *Gleanings from the Writings of Bahá'u'lláh*, p. 326)

Far, far from Thy glory be what mortal man can affirm of Thee, or attribute unto Thee, or the praise with which he can glorify Thee! Whatever duty Thou hast prescribed unto Thy servants of extolling to the utmost Thy majesty and glory is but a token of Thy grace unto them, that they may be enabled to ascend unto the station conferred upon their own inmost being, the station of the knowledge of their own selves.

(Bahá'u'lláh, *Gleanings from the Writings of Bahá'u'lláh*, p. 4)

They say: 'Where is Paradise, and where is Hell?' Say: 'The one is reunion with Me; the other thine own self...

(Bahá'u'lláh, *Tablets of Bahá'u'lláh*, p. 118)

When God created the Remembrance He presented Him to the assemblage of all created beings upon the altar of His Will. Thereupon the concourse of the angels bowed low in adoration to God, the Peerless, the Incomparable; while Satan waxed proud, refusing to submit to His Remembrance; hence he is identified in the Book of God as the arrogant one and the accursed.[1] Chapter LXVII.

[1 cf. Qur'án 2:32; 38:74-78]
(The Báb, *Selections from the Writings of the Báb*, p. 64)

O SON OF JUSTICE! Whither can a lover go but to the land of his beloved? And what seeker findeth rest away from his heart's desire? To the true lover reunion is life, and separation is death. His breast is void of patience and his heart hath no peace. A myriad lives he would forsake to hasten to the abode of his beloved.

(Bahá'u'lláh, *The Hidden Words*, Persian #4)

O MOVING FORM OF DUST! I desire communion with thee, but thou wouldst put no trust in Me. The sword of thy rebellion hath felled the tree of thy hope. At all times I am near unto thee, but thou art ever far from Me. Imperishable glory I have chosen for thee, yet boundless shame thou hast chosen for thyself. While there is yet time, return, and lose not thy chance.

(Bahá'u'lláh, *The Hidden Words*, Persian #21)

O MY FRIEND IN WORD! Ponder awhile. Hast thou ever heard that friend and foe should abide in one heart? Cast out then the stranger, that the Friend may enter His home.

(Bahá'u'lláh, *The Hidden Words*, Persian #26)

O CHILDREN OF NEGLIGENCE AND PASSION! Ye have suffered My enemy to enter My house and have cast out My friend, for ye have enshrined the love of another than Me in your hearts. Give ear to the sayings of the Friend and turn towards His paradise. Worldly friends, seeking their own good, appear to love one the other, whereas the true Friend hath loved and doth love you for your own sakes; indeed He hath suffered for your guidance countless afflictions. Be not disloyal to such a Friend, nay rather hasten unto Him. Such is the daystar of the word of truth and faithfulness, that hath dawned above the horizon of the pen of the Lord of all names. Open your ears that ye may hearken unto the word of God, the Help in peril, the Self-existent.

(Bahá'u'lláh, *The Hidden Words*, Persian #52)

The one true God hath ever regarded the hearts of men as His own, His exclusive possession -- and this too but as an expression of His all-surpassing mercy, that haply mortal souls may be purged and sanctified from all that pertaineth to the world of dust and gain admittance into the realms of eternity.

(Bahá'u'lláh, *The Summons of the Lord of Hosts*, p. 110)

Hearken ye to the Call of this wronged One, and magnify ye the name of the one true God, and adorn yourselves with the ornament of His remembrance, and illumine your hearts with the light of His love. This is the key that unlocketh the hearts of men, the burnish that shall cleanse the souls of all beings. He that is careless of what hath poured out from the finger of the Will of God liveth in manifest error. Amity and rectitude of conduct, rather than dissension and mischief, are the marks of true faith.

(Bahá'u'lláh, *Gleanings from the Writings of Bahá'u'lláh*, p. 204)

Unlock, O people, the gates of the hearts of men with the keys of the remembrance of Him Who is the Remembrance of God and the Source of wisdom amongst you. He hath chosen out of the whole world the hearts of His servants, and made them each a seat for the revelation of His glory. Wherefore, sanctify them from every defilement, that the things for which they were created may be engraven upon them. This indeed is a token of God's bountiful favor.

(Bahá'u'lláh, *Gleanings from the Writings of Bahá'u'lláh*, p. 296)

It is incumbent upon thee, by the permission of God, to cleanse the eye of thine heart from the things of the world, that thou mayest realize the infinitude of divine knowledge, and mayest behold Truth so clearly that thou wilt need no proof to demonstrate His reality, nor any evidence to bear witness unto His testimony.

(Bahá'u'lláh, *The Kitáb-i-Íqán*, p. 90)

How great the number of those holy souls, those essences of justice, who, accused of tyranny, were put to death! And how many embodiments of purity, who showed forth naught but true knowledge and stainless deeds, suffered an agonizing death! Notwithstanding all this, each of these holy beings, up to his last moment, breathed the Name of God, and soared in the realm of submission and resignation. Such was the potency and transmuting influence which He exercised over them, that they ceased to cherish any desire but His will, and wedded their soul to His remembrance.

(Bahá'u'lláh, *The Kitáb-i-Íqán*, p. 234)

Center your thoughts in the Well-Beloved, rather than in your own selves.

(Bahá'u'lláh, *Gleanings from the Writings of Bahá'u'lláh*, p. 167)

…Waft, then, unto me, O my God and my Beloved, from the right hand of Thy mercy and Thy loving-kindness, the holy breaths of Thy favors, that they may draw me away from myself and from the world unto the courts of Thy nearness and Thy presence. Potent art Thou to do what pleaseth Thee. Thou, truly, hast been supreme over all things…

(Bahá'u'lláh, *Prayers and Meditations by Bahá'u'lláh*, p. 310)

Thy name is my healing, O my God, and remembrance of Thee is my remedy. Nearness to Thee is my hope, and love for Thee is my companion. Thy mercy to me is my healing and my succor in both this world and the world to come. Thou, verily, art the All-Bountiful, the All-Knowing, the All-Wise.

(Bahá'u'lláh, *Bahá'í Prayers*, p. 85)

Appendix

Requisites for Spiritual Growth

Bahá'u'lláh has stated quite clearly in His Writings the essential requisites for our spiritual growth, and these are stressed again and again by 'Abdu'l-Bahá in His talks and tablets. One can summarise them briefly in this way:

1. The recital each day of one of the Obligatory Prayers with pure-hearted devotion
2. The regular reading of the Sacred Scriptures, specifically at least each morning and evening, with reverence, attention and thought
3. Prayerful meditation on the teachings, so that we may understand them more deeply, fulfil them more faithfully, and convey them more accurately to others
4. Striving every day to bring our behaviour more into accordance with the high standards that are set forth in the Teachings
5. Teaching the Cause of God
6. Selfless service in the work of the Cause and in the carrying on of our trade or profession

(Compilations, *Lights of Guidance,* p. 540
From a letter written on behalf of the Universal House of
Justice to a National Spiritual Assembly, 1 September 1983)

BIBLIOGRAPHY

'Abdu'l-Bahá. *'Abdu'l-Bahá in London.*

'Abdu'l-Bahá. *Foundations of World Unity.* Wilmette, IL: Bahá'í Publishing Trust, 1968.

'Abdu'l-Bahá. *Paris Talks.* London: Bahá'í Publishing Trust, 1995.

'Abdu'l-Bahá. *Some Answered Questions.* Collected and Translated by Laura Clifford Barney. Wilmette, IL: Bahá'í Publishing Trust: 1987.

'Abdu'l-Bahá. *Tablets of the Divine Plan.* Wilmette, IL: Bahá'í Publishing Trust, 1977.

'Abdu'l-Bahá. *The Promulgation of Universal Peace.* Wilmette, IL: Bahá'í Publishing Trust, 1982.

'Abdu'l-Bahá. *The Secret of Divine Civilization.* Translated from Persian by Marzieh Gail in consultation with Ali-Kuli Khan. Wilmette, IL: Bahá'í Publishing Trust, 1990.

'Abdu'l-Bahá. *Selections from the Writings of 'Abdu'l-Bahá.* Compiled by the Research Department of The Universal House of Justice. Translated by a Committee at the Bahá'í World Centre and by Marzieh Gail. Haifa, Israel: Bahá'í World Centre, 1982.

Bahá'u'lláh. *Epistle to the Son of the Wolf.* Wilmette, IL: Bahá'í Publishing Trust, 1988.

Bahá'u'lláh. *Gems of Divine Mysteries.* Haifa, Israel: Bahá'í World Centre, 2002.

Bahá'u'lláh. *Gleanings from the Writings of Bahá'u'lláh.* Wilmette, IL: Bahá'í Publishing Trust, 1983.

Bahá'u'lláh. *Prayers and Meditations by Bahá'u'lláh.* Wilmette, IL: Bahá'í Publishing Trust, 1987.

Bahá'u'lláh. *Tablets of Bahá'u'lláh.* Universal House of Justice and translated by Habib Taherzadeh with the assistance of a Committee at the Bahá'í World Centre . Wilmette, IL: Bahá'í Publishing Trust, 1988.

Bahá'u'lláh. *The Seven Valleys and the Four Valleys.* Translated by
Marzieh Gail in consultation with Ali Quli Khan . Wilmette, IL:
Bahá'í Publishing Trust, 1986.
Bahá'u'lláh. *The Hidden Words.* Translated by Shoghi Effendi with the
assistance of some English friends . Wilmette, IL: Bahá'í Publish-
ing Trust, 1994.
Bahá'u'lláh. *The Kitáb-i-Aqdas.* Haifa, Israel: Bahá'í World Centre,
1992.
Bahá'u'lláh. *The Kitáb-i-Íqán.* Translated by Shoghi Effendi . Wil-
mette, IL: Bahá'í Publishing Trust, 1983.
Bahá'u'lláh. *The Proclamation of Bahá'u'lláh.* Haifa, Israel: Bahá'í
World Centre, 1967.
Bahá'u'lláh. *The Summons of the Lord of Hosts.* Haifa, Israel: Bahá'í
World Centre, 2002.
Bahá'u'lláh. Bahá'í Prayers, *A Selection of Prayers Revealed by
Bahá'u'lláh, The Báb, and 'Abdul-Bahá.* Wilmette, IL: Bahá'í
Publishing Trust, 1991.
The Báb. *Selections from the Writings of the Báb.* Translated by Habib
Taherzadeh with the assitance of a committee a the Bahá'í World
Centre . Haifa, Israel: Bahá'í World Centre, 1978.
Esslemont, J. E.. *Bahá'u'lláh and the New Era.* Wilmette, IL: Bahá'í
Publishing Trust, 1980.
Lights of Guidance: A Bahá'í Reference File. Compiled by Helen Bas-
sett Hornby. New Delhi, India: Bahaá'í Publishing Trust, 1994.

www.ingramcontent.com/pod-product-compliance
Lightning Source LLC
Chambersburg PA
CBHW031341040426
42443CB00006B/434